SPR

We hope you enjoy this book. Please return or
renew it by the due date.

You can renew it at www.norfolk.gov.uk/libraries or
by using our free library app.

Otherwise you can phone 0344 800 8020 -
please have your library card and PIN ready.

You can sign up for email reminders too.

3|18

NORFOLK ITEM

30129 081 933 195

NORFOLK COUNTY COUNCIL
LIBRARY AND INFORMATION SERVICE

D0569588

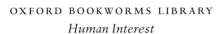

OXFORD BOOKWORMS LIBRARY

Human Interest

The Girl with Red Hair

Starter (250 headwords)

CHRISTINE LINDOP

The Girl
with Red Hair

Illustrated by
Matt Vincent

OXFORD UNIVERSITY PRESS

OXFORD
UNIVERSITY PRESS

Great Clarendon Street, Oxford OX2 6DP

Oxford University Press is a department of the University of Oxford.
It furthers the University's objective of excellence in research, scholarship,
and education by publishing worldwide in

Oxford New York

Auckland Cape Town Dar es Salaam Hong Kong Karachi
Kuala Lumpur Madrid Melbourne Mexico City Nairobi
New Delhi Shanghai Taipei Toronto

With offices in

Argentina Austria Brazil Chile Czech Republic France Greece
Guatemala Hungary Italy Japan Poland Portugal Singapore
South Korea Switzerland Thailand Turkey Ukraine Vietnam

OXFORD and OXFORD ENGLISH are registered trade marks of
Oxford University Press in the UK and in certain other countries

ISBN: 978 0 19 423435 1

A complete recording of this Bookworms edition of
The Girl with Red Hair is available on CD ISBN 978 0 19 423433 7

Printed in China

ACKNOWLEDGEMENTS

Illustrations by: Matt Vincent/Anna Goodson Management

Word count (main text): 1702

For more information on the Oxford Bookworms Library,
visit www.oup.com/bookworms

CONTENTS

Wow!

My name is Mark Sellers. I'm twenty-two years old, and I work in security in Mason's store. You can get everything here – books, TVs, hats, flowers, sandwiches, beds, bicycles . . . It's interesting work, and I like it. Sometimes I walk around in the store, and sometimes I work in the office.

Leon and Shami work in security too. I like working with them.

'Look at this woman,' Leon says. 'Which hat is best for her – blue or black?'

I look at the woman on the screen.

'Oh – the black hat,' I say.

'No!' says Shami. 'The blue hat is nicer.'

We watch and wait. In the end the woman takes the blue hat.

'Hurray!' says Shami. 'You two know nothing about hats.'

Yes, it's interesting work.

Today I'm watching the screens. I'm looking at a man with a big bag. He's got a clock in his hand. He looks around slowly. Now he's got a clock in his bag. The man walks to the door. I talk on my radio. Shami walks quietly behind the man. When he gets to the door, she puts her hand on his arm.

'Please come with me,' she says.
Good. I go back to the screens.

3

And then I see her.

'Wow! Who's that girl?'

'What girl? I can see lots of girls,' Leon says.

Now the picture on the screen is bigger.

'That girl there – with red hair.'

Leon looks at the screen.

'Hmm – yes, she's OK. But who is she? I don't know. Why don't you go and ask her, Mark?'

He laughs and walks away, but I can't stop looking at the screen. Who is that beautiful girl? What is her name? I want to meet her.

Every day I look for the girl with red hair, but I do not see her.

'Where is she?' Leon says every day. 'Where's the girl with red hair, Mark? What's her name?'

'Oh stop it, Leon,' says Shami. 'Mark can dream, can't he?'

I laugh at first, but after three days, I want to hit Leon. Then, suddenly, I see her again.

I am watching a woman with a big bag. And then, there she is – the girl with red hair. She's got green eyes too. But there is a baby with her, a little boy. They are looking at a book about trains.

'Look, Greg,' she says. 'Look at the big train.'

The little boy smiles. He's got red hair and green eyes too. *Her* baby. So – has she got a husband? A boyfriend? I look at her beautiful green eyes again, and then I go back to work. But there are lots of questions in my head.

She comes to the store on Wednesday mornings. She usually arrives at about eleven o'clock.

'How's your girl?' asks Leon.

'She's not my girl,' I say. 'I don't know her name. Her little boy's name is Greg, but she's – the girl with red hair.'

'Well, let's give her a name,' says Leon. 'What do you think, Shami?'

'Hmm – Scarlet! Her name is Scarlet,' says Shami.

'Apples are red,' says Leon. 'Apple is a nice name—'

Then he looks at my face, and runs out the door.

Boohoo

Next Wednesday I am in the store when the girl with red hair comes in with Greg. She stops and looks at a picture. Greg takes his hat off and drops it. I pick up the hat and go over to her.

'Excuse me,' I say. 'Is this your little boy's hat?'

She smiles at me.

'Oh, thank you,' she says. 'Greg, look, it's your hat.'

Greg laughs. She puts out her hand and takes the hat from me. Is she wearing a ring? No, there is no ring on her hand.

Wednesday is the best day of the week, I think.

Ten minutes later, I am near the flowers when Leon speaks to me on my radio.

'Mark, go to the door!' he says. 'You must stop her – the girl with red hair.'

'What? What's happening?' I say.

'Go quickly – now. It's the little boy – he's got one of the red planes.'

Those red planes! Children take them all the time, because they like the colour. Then they get to the door and the alarm rings. Children cry, and their mothers get angry. I hate those planes!

When I get to the door, the alarm is ringing. The girl with red hair is standing there, and her face is red.

'What's happening?' she says.

'Please come back into the store for a minute,' I say.

We go back into the store, and the alarm stops.

'This young man has got the answer, I think. Where's the plane?' I say to Greg.

'Plane,' says Greg, and he waves a little red plane at us.

'Oh, I *am* sorry!' she says.

'It's all right,' I say. 'It happens all the time. Can I have the plane? Good boy!'

'Thank you very much,' says the girl with red hair. But the alarm is ringing again. I must go.

I walk into the office upstairs. Shami is watching the
screens. She stops and looks at my face.

She says nothing, but she smiles. Then she goes back to
work.

I look at the screens too – but I am dreaming.

I'm happy. I'm really happy. But how can I meet her again? I think about this for the next six days, but I can't find any answers. Then it's Wednesday again.

I'm sitting in the office watching the screens. Ten o'clock comes and goes, then eleven o'clock. I can't see her.

I look on every screen in the store. In the end I see her near the door. She's looking at her watch, and talking to Greg. Is she waiting for somebody?

Perhaps she's meeting somebody. Perhaps she's late. Perhaps her mother is coming. Perhaps—

But now she's waving at somebody.

A good-looking man in a black jacket walks up to the girl with red hair and kisses her. Greg laughs, and the man picks him up and kisses him too. Is he the baby's father? Of course he is. Anybody can see that.

I don't want to look, but I can't take my eyes away from the screen. Then they all go down the road, away from the store.

I look around the room. Leon and Shami are in the store, and the room is very quiet. It feels cold.

15

Then Leon and Shami come in. 'Now that's not a happy face,' Shami says. 'What's the matter?'

I tell them. I tell them about the girl with red hair, and Greg, and the good-looking man – and the kiss.

Leon looks at my face and thinks for a minute.

'Look, Mark,' he says. 'It's a dream, that's all. You see a nice girl, you think about her, you talk to her – and one day her boyfriend arrives. Boohoo. You stop dreaming. But there are always more girls.'

'Yes, but—' I say, and then I stop.

'But they're not the girl with red hair, right?' says Leon. 'But she's got a boyfriend. You need a different girl, Mark – a girl without a boyfriend. Why don't you come out with us tonight? We're going to Ocean Blue. It's a wonderful club, and there are lots of nice girls there.'

I don't really want to go, but I don't want to stay at home and do nothing.

'OK, then,' I say.

'Good man,' says Leon. 'See you there at nine.'

Yay!!

The club is dark. There's a lot of noise, and a lot of people, but the music is good.

Leon is there with his girlfriend Ellie. I talk to them and their friends. I'm feeling good. Perhaps tonight I can forget about everything. Leon and Ellie are dancing, so I go to get a drink.

Leon is right about one thing – there are a lot of nice girls at Ocean Blue. Tall girls, interesting girls, girls with black hair, blue hair – and red hair.

Red hair? I'm waiting for my drink, and I'm standing next to the girl with red hair. No, two girls with red hair. Is this really happening?

The girl with red hair looks at me and smiles. 'Just a minute,' she says. 'Don't I know you?'

She's talking to me! Why can't I say anything?

'In the store,' I say at last. 'In Mason's store. With your little boy. And the red plane.'

The girl with red hair laughs.

'Oh, with Greg!' she says. 'I remember. But he isn't *my* baby – he's Claire's. This is my sister Claire – she's his mother.' The second girl with red hair waves at me.

'But I always see you with him,' I say.

'I look after Greg on Wednesday mornings, and we always go to Mason's,' she says. 'Then I meet Claire. Well, usually, that is. But not this week.'

Just then a good-looking man in a black jacket arrives. 'Sorry I'm late,' he says, and kisses Claire. 'Hi, Kate.'

Claire smiles at him, and the girl with red hair says hello. I'm starting to understand. This is Claire's husband, and Greg's father. And the girl with red hair is called Kate.

My face is red.

'Hey, I'm sorry,' I say to Kate. 'It's – well, Greg's got your hair and your eyes. But I can see now. He's got *Claire's* hair and eyes. Of course.'

'It's OK,' Kate says. 'It happens all the time. People say, "Isn't your little boy happy!" And sometimes I just say, "Yes, he is." '

Claire and her husband go off to dance, and I get Kate a drink.

'Here you are, Kate. My name's Mark.'

'Thanks, Mark,' she says. 'So you work in Mason's.'

'Yes,' I say. 'I work in security. I look for little boys with red planes, and girls with red hair.'

'And do you find them?'

'I find lots of little boys with red planes.'

'And the girls?'

'Just one.'

Now I have the answers to my questions. The girl with red hair is Kate. She hasn't got a husband, and she hasn't got a baby. And those green eyes are smiling at me. Yes, Wednesday really is the best day of the week.

GLOSSARY

alarm something that makes a loud noise when
  something is wrong
around in different places
baby a very young child
boyfriend/girlfriend a boy/girl you like and go out with
club a place where you go to dance, listen to music, etc.
dream *(n & v)* to hope for something nice in the future
drop to let something fall
good-looking nice to look at
husband the man that a woman is married to
jacket a short coat
kiss *(v & n)* to touch someone lovingly with your lips
look after to take care of somebody
music what you make when you sing, play the piano, etc.
pick up to take something with your hand
radio a machine that lets you hear somebody's voice
  from far away
ring *(v)* make a sound like a bell (a telephone rings);
  (n) a circle of metal that you wear on your finger
screen the flat part of a TV where you see pictures
security keeping people and places safe
store a big shop that sells a lot of different things
wave *(v)* to move your hand to say hello or goodbye
  to somebody

The Girl with Red Hair

ACTIVITIES

Before Reading

1 **Look at the front and back cover of the book and choose the correct ending for these sentences.**

1 This story is about . . .
   a ☐ work and friends.
   b ☐ love and work.
   c ☐ friends and children.

2 Mark sees the girl . . .
   a ☐ on TV.
   b ☐ in a house.
   c ☐ in a store.

2 **Guess what happens. In the story . . .**   *Yes*   *No*

1 Mark's friends talk to the girl.   ☐   ☐
2 Mark's friends help him.   ☐   ☐
3 the girl does not speak to Mark.   ☐   ☐
4 Mark meets the girl at a club.   ☐   ☐
5 the girl has got a boyfriend.   ☐   ☐
6 the girl starts work in the store.   ☐   ☐

While Reading

1 Read pages 1–4, then answer these questions.

1 Where does Mark work?
2 Who knows most about hats?
3 How does Mark talk to Shami?
4 Who does Mark see on the screen?

2 Read pages 5–8. Are these sentences true (T) or false (F)?

1 Mark wants to meet the girl with red hair.
2 Shami wants to hit Leon.
3 The girl and the baby have got blue eyes.
4 The girl comes to the store on Wednesdays.
5 Leon knows the girl's name.

3 Read pages 9–12 and answer the questions.

Who . . .
1 . . . drops his hat?
2 . . . likes Wednesdays?
3 . . . tells Mark about the plane?
4 . . . has got a red face?
5 . . . is watching the screens in the office?

4 Read pages 13–16. Now answer these questions.

1 Where is Mark on Wednesday morning?
2 What is the girl looking at?
3 Who is the man in the black jacket?
4 Who tells Mark, 'It's a dream'?

5 Read pages 17–19, then match the sentence halves to make four complete sentences.

1 Ocean Blue is a wonderful club . . .
2 Mark doesn't want to go out . . .
3 Mark is feeling good . . .
4 Mark wants to forget about everything . . .

a but he doesn't want to stay at home.
b but then he sees two girls with red hair.
c because he likes the music and the people at the club.
d and there are lots of nice girls there.

6 Guess what happens next in the story.	*Yes*	*No*
1 The two girls are sisters.	☐	☐
2 The girl is the baby's mother.	☐	☐
3 The girl's sister is the baby's mother.	☐	☐
4 The man in the black jacket is the girl's husband.	☐	☐
5 The girl hasn't got a husband.	☐	☐
6 Mark gives the girl some flowers.	☐	☐

After Reading

1 **What do you know about Kate and Mark? Choose the right words for each person, and then write a description.**

> *work / Mason's store*
> *red hair / green eyes*
> *twenty-two years old*
> *sister Claire / little boy Greg*
> *work / Leon and Shami*
> *like working / security*
> *look after Greg / Wednesdays*

2 **Put these sentences in the correct order. Number them 1–10.**

a ☐ The girl leaves with the man and Greg.

b ☐ The good-looking man (Claire's husband) arrives.

c ☐ Leon says, 'Come with us to Ocean Blue.'

d ☐ Mark meets her sister Claire.

e ☐ Mark tells his friends about the boyfriend.

f ☐ At the club, Mark sees two girls with red hair.

g ☐ Mark gets Kate a drink, and she smiles at him.

h ☐ A good-looking man meets her and kisses her.

i ☐ The girl with red hair tells Mark about her family.

j ☐ The girl is waiting by the door of the store.

3 Who says this? Who do they say it to?

1 'You two know nothing about hats.'
2 'Look at the big train.'
3 'Apple is a nice name—'
4 'Oh, I *am* sorry!'
5 'Sorry I'm late.'
6 'Just one.'

4 Complete this summary of the story. Use these words:

club   door   every   feels   good-looking
husband   kisses   plane   sorry   stops

Mark sees a beautiful girl with red hair in Mason's store. She comes to the store _____ Wednesday with a little boy called Greg. One day Greg takes a little _____ , and Mark _____ the girl and Greg near the door. Her face is red and she is very _____ . The next Wednesday a _____ man meets her and Greg at the _____ of the store and _____ them. Mark is not happy. That night he goes to the Ocean Blue _____ . There he meets the girl with red hair, Kate, and her sister Claire. Greg is Claire's baby, and the good-looking man is her _____ . Kate hasn't got a boyfriend. Mark _____ very good.

ABOUT THE AUTHOR

Christine Lindop was born in New Zealand and taught English in France and Spain before settling in Great Britain. She has written more than twenty books, including several Bookworms: *Red Roses*, *Sally's Phone* (Starter), *Ned Kelly: A True Story* (Stage 1), and *Australia and New Zealand* (Stage 3). She has also adapted *Goldfish* (Stage 3) and edited *A Tangled Web* for the Oxford Bookworms Collection. She has worked on many other Oxford readers series as both an editor and a writer. In her free time she likes reading, watching films, gardening, and cooking.

OXFORD BOOKWORMS LIBRARY

Classics • Crime & Mystery • Factfiles • Fantasy & Horror
Human Interest • Playscripts • Thriller & Adventure
True Stories • World Stories

The OXFORD BOOKWORMS LIBRARY provides enjoyable reading in English, with a wide range of classic and modern fiction, non-fiction, and plays. It includes original and adapted texts in seven carefully graded language stages, which take learners from beginner to advanced level. An overview is given on the next pages.

All Stage 1 titles are available as audio recordings, as well as over eighty other titles from Starter to Stage 6. All Starters and many titles at Stages 1 to 4 are specially recommended for younger learners. Every Bookworm is illustrated, and Starters and Factfiles have full-colour illustrations.

The OXFORD BOOKWORMS LIBRARY also offers extensive support. Each book contains an introduction to the story, notes about the author, a glossary, and activities. Additional resources include tests and worksheets, and answers for these and for the activities in the books. There is advice on running a class library, using audio recordings, and the many ways of using Oxford Bookworms in reading programmes. Resource materials are available on the website <www.oup.com/bookworms>.

The *Oxford Bookworms Collection* is a series for advanced learners. It consists of volumes of short stories by well-known authors, both classic and modern. Texts are not abridged or adapted in any way, but carefully selected to be accessible to the advanced student.

You can find details and a full list of titles in the *Oxford Bookworms Library Catalogue* and *Oxford English Language Teaching Catalogues*, and on the website <www.oup.com/bookworms>.

THE OXFORD BOOKWORMS LIBRARY
GRADING AND SAMPLE EXTRACTS

STARTER • 250 HEADWORDS

present simple – present continuous – imperative –
can/cannot, must – *going to* (future) – simple gerunds …

Her phone is ringing – but where is it?

Sally gets out of bed and looks in her bag. No phone. She looks under the bed. No phone. Then she looks behind the door. There is her phone. Sally picks up her phone and answers it. *Sally's Phone*

STAGE 1 • 400 HEADWORDS

… past simple – coordination with *and, but, or* –
subordination with *before, after, when, because, so* …

I knew him in Persia. He was a famous builder and I worked with him there. For a time I was his friend, but not for long. When he came to Paris, I came after him – I wanted to watch him. He was a very clever, very dangerous man. *The Phantom of the Opera*

STAGE 2 • 700 HEADWORDS

… present perfect – *will* (future) – *(don't) have to, must not, could* –
comparison of adjectives – simple *if* clauses – past continuous –
tag questions – *ask/tell* + infinitive …

While I was writing these words in my diary, I decided what to do. I must try to escape. I shall try to get down the wall outside. The window is high above the ground, but I have to try. I shall take some of the gold with me – if I escape, perhaps it will be helpful later. *Dracula*

STAGE 3 • 1000 HEADWORDS

… should, may – present perfect continuous – *used to* – past perfect
– causative – relative clauses – indirect statements …

Of course, it was most important that no one should see
Colin, Mary, or Dickon entering the secret garden. So Colin
gave orders to the gardeners that they must all keep away
from that part of the garden in future. *The Secret Garden*

STAGE 4 • 1400 HEADWORDS

… past perfect continuous – passive (simple forms) –
would conditional clauses – indirect questions –
relatives with *where/when* – gerunds after prepositions/phrases …

I was glad. Now Hyde could not show his face to the world
again. If he did, every honest man in London would be
proud to report him to the police. *Dr Jekyll and Mr Hyde*

STAGE 5 • 1800 HEADWORDS

… future continuous – future perfect –
passive (modals, continuous forms) –
would have conditional clauses – modals + perfect infinitive …

If he had spoken Estella's name, I would have hit him. I was so
angry with him, and so depressed about my future, that I could
not eat the breakfast. Instead I went straight to the old house.
Great Expectations

STAGE 6 • 2500 HEADWORDS

… passive (infinitives, gerunds) – advanced modal meanings –
clauses of concession, condition

When I stepped up to the piano, I was confident. It was as if
I knew that the prodigy side of me really did exist. And when I
started to play, I was so caught up in how lovely I looked that I
didn't worry how I would sound. *The Joy Luck Club*

Red Roses
CHRISTINE LINDOP

'Who is the man with the roses in his hand?' thinks Anna. 'I want to meet him.'

'Who is the girl with the guitar?' thinks Will. 'I like her. I want to meet her.'

But they do not meet.

'There are lots of men!' says Anna's friend Vicki, but Anna cannot forget Will. And then one rainy day . . .

Sally's Phone
CHRISTINE LINDOP

Sally is always running – and she has her phone with her all the time: at home, on the train, at work, at lunchtime, and at the shops.

But then one afternoon suddenly she has a different phone . . . and it changes her life.

Give us the Money

MAEVE CLARKE

'Every day is the same. Nothing exciting ever happens to me,' thinks Adam one boring Monday morning. But today is not the same. When he helps a beautiful young woman because some men want to take her bag, life gets exciting and very, very dangerous.

Orca

PHILLIP BURROWS AND MARK FOSTER

When Tonya and her friends decide to sail around the world they want to see exciting things and visit exciting places.

But one day, they meet an orca – a killer whale – one of the most dangerous animals in the sea. And life gets a little too exciting.

Ned Kelly: A True Story

CHRISTINE LINDOP

When he was a boy, he was poor and hungry. When he was a young man, he was still poor and still hungry. He learnt how to steal horses, he learnt how to fight, he learnt how to live – outside the law. Australia in the 1870s was a hard, wild place. Rich people had land, poor people didn't. So the rich got richer, and the poor stayed poor.

Some say Ned Kelly was a bad man. Some say he was a good man but the law was bad. This is the true story of Australia's most famous outlaw.

Pocahontas

Retold by Tim Vicary

A beautiful young Indian girl, and a brave Englishman. Black eyes, and blue eyes. A friendly smile, a laugh, a look of love . . . But this is North America in 1607, and love is not easy. The girl is the daughter of King Powhatan, and the Englishman is a white man. And the Indians of Virginia do not want the white men in their beautiful country.

This is the famous story of Pocahontas, and her love for the Englishman John Smith.